A N

Somebody Is On Your Mind

From Executive Coach, Speaker,
Personal & Professional Development Expert,
and #1 Bestselling Author
KIM ROGNE
with #1 Bestselling Author Reji Laberje

Author: Kim Rogne
Contributor: Reji Laberje

From Lucy's Lantern Literature & Jeri Shepherd Books www.RedWritesBooks.com

Learn more about the authors, Kim Rogne and Reji Laberje, human, non-AI creatives, at: www.KimRogne.com & www.RedWritesBooks.com respectively.

You were on my mind.

_____

I thought of you because:

_____

_____

_____

_____

The action I'll take
because of this is:

_____

_____

_____

_____

_____

You were on my mind.

_____

I thought of you because:

_____

_____

_____

The action I'll take
because of this is:

_____

_____

_____

_____

You were on my mind.

_____

I thought of you because:

_____

_____

_____

_____

The action I'll take
because of this is:

_____

_____

_____

_____

_____

You were on my mind.

_____

I thought of you because:

_____

_____

_____

_____

The action I'll take
because of this is:

_____

_____

_____

_____

You were on my mind.

_____

I thought of you because:

_____

_____

_____

The action I'll take
because of this is:

_____

_____

_____

_____

_____

You were on my mind.

_____

I thought of you because:

_____

_____

_____

_____

The action I'll take
because of this is:

_____

_____

_____

_____

You were on my mind.

_____

I thought of you because:

_____

_____

_____

_____

The action I'll take
because of this is:

_____

_____

_____

_____

_____

You were on my mind.

_____

I thought of you because:

_____

_____

_____

_____

The action I'll take
because of this is:

_____

_____

_____

_____

_____

You were on my mind.

_____

I thought of you because:

_____

_____

_____

The action I'll take
because of this is:

_____

_____

_____

_____

You were on my mind.

_____

I thought of you because:

_____
_____
_____
_____

The action I'll take
because of this is:

_____
_____
_____
_____
_____

You were on my mind.

_____

I thought of you because:

_____
_____
_____
_____

The action I'll take
because of this is:

_____
_____
_____
_____
_____

You were on my mind.

_____

I thought of you because:

_____
_____
_____
_____

The action I'll take
because of this is:

_____
_____
_____
_____

You were on my mind.

_____

I thought of you because:

_____

_____

_____

_____

The action I'll take
because of this is:

_____

_____

_____

_____

You were on my mind.

_____

I thought of you because:

_____

_____

_____

_____

The action I'll take
because of this is:

_____

_____

_____

_____

You were on my mind.

_____

I thought of you because:

_____

_____

_____

The action I'll take
because of this is:

_____

_____

_____

_____

_____

You were on my mind.

_____

I thought of you because:

_____
_____
_____
_____

The action I'll take
because of this is:

_____
_____
_____
_____
_____

You were on my mind.

_____

I thought of you because:

_____

_____

_____

_____

The action I'll take
because of this is:

_____

_____

_____

_____

_____

You were on my mind.

_____

I thought of you because:

_____

_____

_____

_____

The action I'll take
because of this is:

_____

_____

_____

_____

_____

You were on my mind.

_____

I thought of you because:

_____

_____

_____

_____

The action I'll take
because of this is:

_____

_____

_____

_____

_____

You were on my mind.

_____

I thought of you because:

_____

_____

_____

The action I'll take
because of this is:

_____

_____

_____

_____

You were on my mind.

_____

I thought of you because:

_____

_____

_____

_____

The action I'll take
because of this is:

_____

_____

_____

_____

_____

You were on my mind.

_____

I thought of you because:

_____

_____

_____

The action I'll take
because of this is:

_____

_____

_____

_____

You were on my mind.

_____

I thought of you because:

_____

_____

_____

_____

The action I'll take
because of this is:

_____

_____

_____

_____

_____

You were on my mind.

_____

I thought of you because:

_____

_____

_____

The action I'll take
because of this is:

_____

_____

_____

_____

You were on my mind.

_____

I thought of you because:

_____

_____

_____

_____

The action I'll take
because of this is:

_____

_____

_____

_____

_____

You were on my mind.

_____

I thought of you because:

_____

_____

_____

_____

The action I'll take
because of this is:

_____

_____

_____

_____

_____

You were on my mind.

_____

I thought of you because:

_____

_____

_____

The action I'll take
because of this is:

_____

_____

_____

_____

_____

You were on my mind.

_____

I thought of you because:

_____

_____

_____

_____

The action I'll take
because of this is:

_____

_____

_____

_____

_____

You were on my mind.

_____

I thought of you because:

_____

_____

_____

_____

The action I'll take
because of this is:

_____

_____

_____

_____

_____

You were on my mind.

_____

I thought of you because:

_____

_____

_____

The action I'll take
because of this is:

_____

_____

_____

_____

You were on my mind.

_____

I thought of you because:

_____

_____

_____

_____

The action I'll take
because of this is:

_____

_____

_____

_____

_____

You were on my mind.

_____

I thought of you because:

_____

_____

_____

_____

The action I'll take
because of this is:

_____

_____

_____

_____

_____

You were on my mind.

_____

I thought of you because:

_____

_____

_____

_____

The action I'll take
because of this is:

_____

_____

_____

_____

You were on my mind.

_____

I thought of you because:

_____

_____

_____

_____

The action I'll take
because of this is:

_____

_____

_____

_____

_____

You were on my mind.

_____

I thought of you because:

_____

_____

_____

_____

The action I'll take
because of this is:

_____

_____

_____

_____

_____

You were on my mind.

_____

I thought of you because:

_____

_____

_____

_____

The action I'll take
because of this is:

_____

_____

_____

_____

_____

You were on my mind.

_____

I thought of you because:

_____

_____

_____

_____

The action I'll take
because of this is:

_____

_____

_____

_____

_____

You were on my mind.

_____

I thought of you because:

_____

_____

_____

_____

The action I'll take
because of this is:

_____

_____

_____

_____

_____

You were on my mind.

_____

I thought of you because:

_____

_____

_____

_____

The action I'll take
because of this is:

_____

_____

_____

_____

_____

You were on my mind.

_____

I thought of you because:

_____

_____

_____

_____

The action I'll take
because of this is:

_____

_____

_____

_____

You were on my mind.

_____

I thought of you because:

_____

_____

_____

_____

The action I'll take
because of this is:

_____

_____

_____

_____

_____

You were on my mind.

_____

I thought of you because:

_____
_____
_____
_____

The action I'll take
because of this is:

_____
_____
_____
_____
_____

You were on my mind.

_____

I thought of you because:

_____

_____

_____

_____

The action I'll take
because of this is:

_____

_____

_____

_____

_____

You were on my mind.

_____

I thought of you because:

_____

_____

_____

The action I'll take
because of this is:

_____

_____

_____

_____

You were on my mind.

_____

I thought of you because:

_____

_____

_____

_____

The action I'll take
because of this is:

_____

_____

_____

_____

You were on my mind.

_____

I thought of you because:

_____

_____

_____

The action I'll take
because of this is:

_____

_____

_____

_____

You were on my mind.

_____

I thought of you because:

_____

_____

_____

_____

The action I'll take
because of this is:

_____

_____

_____

_____

_____

You were on my mind.

_____

I thought of you because:

_____

_____

_____

_____

The action I'll take
because of this is:

_____

_____

_____

_____

_____

You were on my mind.

_____

I thought of you because:

_____

_____

_____

_____

The action I'll take
because of this is:

_____

_____

_____

_____

_____

You were on my mind.

_____

I thought of you because:

_____

_____

_____

The action I'll take
because of this is:

_____

_____

_____

_____

You were on my mind.

_____

I thought of you because:

_____

_____

_____

_____

The action I'll take
because of this is:

_____

_____

_____

_____

_____

You were on my mind.

_____

I thought of you because:

_____
_____
_____
_____

The action I'll take
because of this is:

_____
_____
_____
_____
_____

You were on my mind.

_____

I thought of you because:

_____

_____

_____

The action I'll take
because of this is:

_____

_____

_____

_____

You were on my mind.

_____

I thought of you because:

_____

_____

_____

_____

The action I'll take
because of this is:

_____

_____

_____

_____

_____

You were on my mind.

_____

I thought of you because:

_____

_____

_____

The action I'll take
because of this is:

_____

_____

_____

_____

You were on my mind.

_____

I thought of you because:

_____

_____

_____

The action I'll take
because of this is:

_____

_____

_____

_____

You were on my mind.

_____

I thought of you because:

_____

_____

_____

_____

The action I'll take
because of this is:

_____

_____

_____

_____

_____

You were on my mind.

_____

I thought of you because:

_____

_____

_____

The action I'll take
because of this is:

_____

_____

_____

_____

You were on my mind.

_____

I thought of you because:

_____

_____

_____

The action I'll take
because of this is:

_____

_____

_____

_____

You were on my mind.

_____

I thought of you because:

_____

_____

_____

_____

The action I'll take
because of this is:

_____

_____

_____

_____

You were on my mind.

_____

I thought of you because:

_____

_____

_____

The action I'll take
because of this is:

_____

_____

_____

_____

You were on my mind.

_____

I thought of you because:

_____

_____

_____

_____

The action I'll take
because of this is:

_____

_____

_____

_____

_____

You were on my mind.

_____

I thought of you because:

_____

_____

_____

_____

The action I'll take
because of this is:

_____

_____

_____

_____

_____

You were on my mind.

_____

I thought of you because:

_____

_____

_____

The action I'll take
because of this is:

_____

_____

_____

_____

You were on my mind.

_____

I thought of you because:

_____

_____

_____

_____

The action I'll take
because of this is:

_____

_____

_____

_____

_____

You were on my mind.

_____

I thought of you because:

_____

_____

_____

The action I'll take
because of this is:

_____

_____

_____

_____

You were on my mind.

_____

I thought of you because:

_____

_____

_____

_____

The action I'll take
because of this is:

_____

_____

_____

_____

_____

You were on my mind.

_____

I thought of you because:

_____

_____

_____

_____

The action I'll take
because of this is:

_____

_____

_____

_____

_____

You were on my mind.

_____

I thought of you because:

_____
_____
_____
_____

The action I'll take
because of this is:

_____
_____
_____
_____
_____

You were on my mind.

_____

I thought of you because:

_____

_____

_____

_____

The action I'll take because of this is:

_____

_____

_____

_____

_____

You were on my mind.

_____

I thought of you because:

_____

_____

_____

_____

The action I'll take
because of this is:

_____

_____

_____

_____

_____

You were on my mind.

_____

I thought of you because:

_____

_____

_____

_____

The action I'll take
because of this is:

_____

_____

_____

_____

_____

You were on my mind.

_____

I thought of you because:

_____

_____

_____

_____

The action I'll take
because of this is:

_____

_____

_____

_____

You were on my mind.

_____

I thought of you because:

_____

_____

_____

_____

The action I'll take
because of this is:

_____

_____

_____

_____

_____

You were on my mind.

_____

I thought of you because:

_____

_____

_____

_____

The action I'll take
because of this is:

_____

_____

_____

_____

_____

You were on my mind.

_____

I thought of you because:

_____

_____

_____

The action I'll take
because of this is:

_____

_____

_____

_____

_____

You were on my mind.

_____

I thought of you because:

_____

_____

_____

_____

The action I'll take
because of this is:

_____

_____

_____

_____

_____

You were on my mind.

_____

I thought of you because:

_____
_____
_____
_____

The action I'll take
because of this is:

_____
_____
_____
_____
_____

You were on my mind.

_____

I thought of you because:

_____

_____

_____

_____

The action I'll take
because of this is:

_____

_____

_____

_____

You were on my mind.

_____

I thought of you because:

_____

_____

_____

_____

The action I'll take
because of this is:

_____

_____

_____

_____

_____

You were on my mind.

_____

I thought of you because:

_____
_____
_____
_____

The action I'll take
because of this is:

_____
_____
_____
_____
_____

You were on my mind.

_____

I thought of you because:

_____

_____

_____

_____

The action I'll take because of this is:

_____

_____

_____

_____

_____

You were on my mind.

_____

I thought of you because:

_____
_____
_____
_____

The action I'll take
because of this is:

_____
_____
_____
_____

You were on my mind.

_____

I thought of you because:

_____

_____

_____

_____

The action I'll take
because of this is:

_____

_____

_____

_____

_____

You were on my mind.

_____

I thought of you because:

_____

_____

_____

_____

The action I'll take
because of this is:

_____

_____

_____

_____

_____

You were on my mind.

_____

I thought of you because:

_____

_____

_____

_____

The action I'll take
because of this is:

_____

_____

_____

_____

_____

You were on my mind.

_____

I thought of you because:

_____
_____
_____
_____

The action I'll take
because of this is:

_____
_____
_____
_____

You were on my mind.

_____

I thought of you because:

_____
_____
_____
_____

The action I'll take
because of this is:

_____
_____
_____
_____

You were on my mind.

_____

I thought of you because:

_____

_____

_____

_____

The action I'll take
because of this is:

_____

_____

_____

_____

_____

You were on my mind.

_____

I thought of you because:

_____

_____

_____

The action I'll take
because of this is:

_____

_____

_____

_____

_____

You were on my mind.

_____

I thought of you because:

_____

_____

_____

_____

The action I'll take
because of this is:

_____

_____

_____

_____

You were on my mind.

_____

I thought of you because:

_____

_____

_____

The action I'll take
because of this is:

_____

_____

_____

_____

You were on my mind.

_____

I thought of you because:

_____

_____

_____

_____

The action I'll take
because of this is:

_____

_____

_____

_____

_____

You were on my mind.

_____

I thought of you because:

_____
_____
_____
_____

The action I'll take
because of this is:

_____
_____
_____
_____
_____

You were on my mind.

_____

I thought of you because:

_____

_____

_____

_____

The action I'll take
because of this is:

_____

_____

_____

_____

_____

You were on my mind.

_____

I thought of you because:

_____

_____

_____

_____

The action I'll take
because of this is:

_____

_____

_____

_____

_____

You were on my mind.

_____

I thought of you because:

_____

_____

_____

_____

The action I'll take
because of this is:

_____

_____

_____

_____

_____

You were on my mind.

_____

I thought of you because:

_____

_____

_____

_____

The action I'll take
because of this is:

_____

_____

_____

_____

_____

You were on my mind.

_____

I thought of you because:

_____

_____

_____

_____

The action I'll take
because of this is:

_____

_____

_____

_____

_____

You were on my mind.

_____

I thought of you because:

_____

_____

_____

_____

The action I'll take
because of this is:

_____

_____

_____

_____

_____

You were on my mind.

_____

I thought of you because:

_____

_____

_____

The action I'll take
because of this is:

_____

_____

_____

_____

You were on my mind.

_____

I thought of you because:

_____

_____

_____

The action I'll take
because of this is:

_____

_____

_____

_____

You were on my mind.

_____

I thought of you because:

_____

_____

_____

_____

The action I'll take
because of this is:

_____

_____

_____

_____

_____

You were on my mind.

_____

I thought of you because:

_____

_____

_____

The action I'll take
because of this is:

_____

_____

_____

_____

You were on my mind.

_____

I thought of you because:

_____

_____

_____

_____

The action I'll take
because of this is:

_____

_____

_____

_____

You were on my mind.

_____

I thought of you because:

_____

_____

_____

_____

The action I'll take
because of this is:

_____

_____

_____

_____

_____

You were on my mind.

_____

I thought of you because:

_____

_____

_____

_____

The action I'll take
because of this is:

_____

_____

_____

_____

_____

You were on my mind.

_____

I thought of you because:

_____

_____

_____

The action I'll take
because of this is:

_____

_____

_____

_____

You were on my mind.

_____

I thought of you because:

_____

_____

_____

_____

The action I'll take
because of this is:

_____

_____

_____

_____

_____

You were on my mind.

_____

I thought of you because:

_____

_____

_____

_____

The action I'll take
because of this is:

_____

_____

_____

_____

_____

You were on my mind.

_____

I thought of you because:

_____

_____

_____

The action I'll take
because of this is:

_____

_____

_____

_____

You were on my mind.

_____

I thought of you because:

_____

_____

_____

_____

The action I'll take
because of this is:

_____

_____

_____

_____

_____

You were on my mind.

_____

I thought of you because:

_____

_____

_____

_____

The action I'll take
because of this is:

_____

_____

_____

_____

_____

You were on my mind.

_____

I thought of you because:

_____

_____

_____

The action I'll take
because of this is:

_____

_____

_____

_____

You were on my mind.

_____

I thought of you because:

_____

_____

_____

The action I'll take
because of this is:

_____

_____

_____

_____

You were on my mind.

_____

I thought of you because:

_____

_____

_____

_____

The action I'll take
because of this is:

_____

_____

_____

_____

_____

You were on my mind.

_____

I thought of you because:

_____

_____

_____

_____

The action I'll take
because of this is:

_____

_____

_____

_____

_____

You were on my mind.

_____

I thought of you because:

_____

_____

_____

_____

The action I'll take
because of this is:

_____

_____

_____

_____

_____

You were on my mind.

_____

I thought of you because:

_____

_____

_____

The action I'll take
because of this is:

_____

_____

_____

_____

You were on my mind.

_____

I thought of you because:

_____

_____

_____

The action I'll take
because of this is:

_____

_____

_____

_____

You were on my mind.

_____

I thought of you because:

_____

_____

_____

The action I'll take
because of this is:

_____

_____

_____

_____

You were on my mind.

_____

I thought of you because:

_____

_____

_____

The action I'll take
because of this is:

_____

_____

_____

_____

You were on my mind.

_____

I thought of you because:

_____

_____

_____

_____

The action I'll take
because of this is:

_____

_____

_____

_____

_____

You were on my mind.

_____

I thought of you because:

_____

_____

_____

_____

The action I'll take
because of this is:

_____

_____

_____

_____

_____

You were on my mind.

_____

I thought of you because:

_____

_____

_____

_____

The action I'll take
because of this is:

_____

_____

_____

_____

_____

You were on my mind.

_____

I thought of you because:

_____

_____

_____

_____

The action I'll take
because of this is:

_____

_____

_____

_____

_____

You were on my mind.

_____

I thought of you because:

_____
_____
_____
_____

The action I'll take
because of this is:

_____
_____
_____
_____
_____

You were on my mind.

_____

I thought of you because:

_____

_____

_____

_____

The action I'll take
because of this is:

_____

_____

_____

_____

_____

You were on my mind.

_____

I thought of you because:

_____

_____

_____

The action I'll take
because of this is:

_____

_____

_____

_____

You were on my mind.

_____

I thought of you because:

_____

_____

_____

The action I'll take
because of this is:

_____

_____

_____

_____

_____

You were on my mind.

_____

I thought of you because:

_____

_____

_____

The action I'll take
because of this is:

_____

_____

_____

_____

You were on my mind.

_____

I thought of you because:

_____

_____

_____

_____

The action I'll take
because of this is:

_____

_____

_____

_____

_____

You were on my mind.

_____

I thought of you because:

_____

_____

_____

_____

The action I'll take
because of this is:

_____

_____

_____

_____

You were on my mind.

_____

I thought of you because:

_____

_____

_____

The action I'll take
because of this is:

_____

_____

_____

_____

You were on my mind.

_____

I thought of you because:

_____

_____

_____

_____

The action I'll take
because of this is:

_____

_____

_____

_____

_____

You were on my mind.

_____

I thought of you because:

_____

_____

_____

_____

The action I'll take
because of this is:

_____

_____

_____

_____

_____

You were on my mind.

_____

I thought of you because:

_____

_____

_____

_____

The action I'll take
because of this is:

_____

_____

_____

_____

You were on my mind.

_____

I thought of you because:

_____

_____

_____

The action I'll take
because of this is:

_____

_____

_____

_____

_____

You were on my mind.

_____

I thought of you because:

_____

_____

_____

_____

The action I'll take
because of this is:

_____

_____

_____

_____

_____

You were on my mind.

_____

I thought of you because:

_____

_____

_____

The action I'll take
because of this is:

_____

_____

_____

_____

_____

You were on my mind.

_____

I thought of you because:

_____

_____

_____

_____

The action I'll take
because of this is:

_____

_____

_____

_____

_____

You were on my mind.

_____

I thought of you because:

_____

_____

_____

_____

The action I'll take
because of this is:

_____

_____

_____

_____

_____

You were on my mind.

_____

I thought of you because:

_____

_____

_____

_____

The action I'll take
because of this is:

_____

_____

_____

_____

You were on my mind.

_____

I thought of you because:

_____

_____

_____

_____

The action I'll take
because of this is:

_____

_____

_____

_____

_____

You were on my mind.

_____

I thought of you because:

_____

_____

_____

_____

The action I'll take
because of this is:

_____

_____

_____

_____

_____

You were on my mind.

_____

I thought of you because:

_____

_____

_____

The action I'll take
because of this is:

_____

_____

_____

_____

_____

You were on my mind.

_____

I thought of you because:

_____

_____

_____

_____

The action I'll take
because of this is:

_____

_____

_____

_____

You were on my mind.

_____

I thought of you because:

_____

_____

_____

The action I'll take
because of this is:

_____

_____

_____

_____

_____

You were on my mind.

_____

I thought of you because:

_____

_____

_____

_____

The action I'll take
because of this is:

_____

_____

_____

_____

_____

You were on my mind.

_____

I thought of you because:

_____

_____

_____

The action I'll take
because of this is:

_____

_____

_____

_____

You were on my mind.

_____

I thought of you because:

_____

_____

_____

_____

The action I'll take
because of this is:

_____

_____

_____

_____

_____

You were on my mind.

_____

I thought of you because:

_____

_____

_____

_____

The action I'll take
because of this is:

_____

_____

_____

_____

_____

You were on my mind.

_____

I thought of you because:

_____

_____

_____

The action I'll take
because of this is:

_____

_____

_____

_____

You were on my mind.

_____

I thought of you because:

_____
_____
_____
_____

The action I'll take
because of this is:

_____
_____
_____
_____
_____

You were on my mind.

_____

I thought of you because:

_____

_____

_____

_____

The action I'll take
because of this is:

_____

_____

_____

_____

_____

You were on my mind.

_____

I thought of you because:

_____

_____

_____

The action I'll take
because of this is:

_____

_____

_____

_____

_____

You were on my mind.

_____

I thought of you because:

_____

_____

_____

_____

The action I'll take
because of this is:

_____

_____

_____

_____

_____

You were on my mind.

_____

I thought of you because:

_____
_____
_____
_____

The action I'll take
because of this is:

_____
_____
_____
_____
_____

You were on my mind.

_____

I thought of you because:

_____

_____

_____

_____

The action I'll take
because of this is:

_____

_____

_____

_____

_____

You were on my mind.

_____

I thought of you because:

_____

_____

_____

_____

The action I'll take
because of this is:

_____

_____

_____

_____

_____

You were on my mind.

_____

I thought of you because:

_____

_____

_____

_____

The action I'll take
because of this is:

_____

_____

_____

_____

You were on my mind.

_____

I thought of you because:

_____

_____

_____

The action I'll take
because of this is:

_____

_____

_____

_____

_____

You were on my mind.

_____

I thought of you because:

_____

_____

_____

_____

*The action I'll take
because of this is:*

_____

_____

_____

_____

_____

You were on my mind.

_____

I thought of you because:

_____

_____

_____

_____

The action I'll take
because of this is:

_____

_____

_____

_____

_____

You were on my mind.

_____

I thought of you because:

_____

_____

_____

_____

The action I'll take
because of this is:

_____

_____

_____

_____

You were on my mind.

_____

I thought of you because:

_____

_____

_____

The action I'll take
because of this is:

_____

_____

_____

_____

You were on my mind.

_____

I thought of you because:

_____
_____
_____
_____

The action I'll take
because of this is:

_____
_____
_____
_____
_____

You were on my mind.

_____

I thought of you because:

_____

_____

_____

_____

The action I'll take
because of this is:

_____

_____

_____

_____

You were on my mind.

_____

I thought of you because:

_____

_____

_____

The action I'll take
because of this is:

_____

_____

_____

_____

You were on my mind.

_____

I thought of you because:

_____

_____

_____

The action I'll take
because of this is:

_____

_____

_____

_____

_____

You were on my mind.

_____

I thought of you because:

_____
_____
_____
_____

The action I'll take
because of this is:

_____
_____
_____
_____

You were on my mind.

_____

I thought of you because:

_____

_____

_____

The action I'll take
because of this is:

_____

_____

_____

_____

You were on my mind.

_____

I thought of you because:

_____

_____

_____

The action I'll take
because of this is:

_____

_____

_____

_____

You were on my mind.

_____

I thought of you because:

_____

_____

_____

The action I'll take
because of this is:

_____

_____

_____

_____

_____

You were on my mind.

_____

I thought of you because:

_____
_____
_____
_____

The action I'll take
because of this is:

_____
_____
_____
_____
_____

You were on my mind.

_____

I thought of you because:

_____

_____

_____

_____

The action I'll take
because of this is:

_____

_____

_____

_____

_____

You were on my mind.

_____

I thought of you because:

_____

_____

_____

The action I'll take
because of this is:

_____

_____

_____

_____

_____

You were on my mind.

_____

I thought of you because:

_____

_____

_____

_____

The action I'll take
because of this is:

_____

_____

_____

_____

_____

You were on my mind.

_____

I thought of you because:

_____

_____

_____

_____

The action I'll take
because of this is:

_____

_____

_____

_____

_____

You were on my mind.

_____

I thought of you because:

_____
_____
_____
_____

The action I'll take
because of this is:

_____
_____
_____
_____
_____

You were on my mind.

_____

I thought of you because:

_____

_____

_____

_____

The action I'll take
because of this is:

_____

_____

_____

_____

You were on my mind.

_____

I thought of you because:

_____

_____

_____

The action I'll take
because of this is:

_____

_____

_____

_____

You were on my mind.

_____

I thought of you because:

_____

_____

_____

The action I'll take
because of this is:

_____

_____

_____

_____

You were on my mind.

_____

I thought of you because:

_____

_____

_____

_____

The action I'll take
because of this is:

_____

_____

_____

_____

_____

You were on my mind.

_____

I thought of you because:

_____

_____

_____

_____

The action I'll take
because of this is:

_____

_____

_____

_____

_____

You were on my mind.

_____

I thought of you because:

_____

_____

_____

_____

The action I'll take
because of this is:

_____

_____

_____

_____

_____

You were on my mind.

_____

I thought of you because:

_____

_____

_____

The action I'll take
because of this is:

_____

_____

_____

_____

You were on my mind.

_____

I thought of you because:

_____

_____

_____

The action I'll take
because of this is:

_____

_____

_____

_____

_____

You were on my mind.

_____

I thought of you because:

_____

_____

_____

_____

The action I'll take
because of this is:

_____

_____

_____

_____

_____

You were on my mind.

_____

I thought of you because:

_____

_____

_____

The action I'll take
because of this is:

_____

_____

_____

_____

_____

You were on my mind.

_____

I thought of you because:

_____

_____

_____

_____

The action I'll take
because of this is:

_____

_____

_____

_____

You were on my mind.

_____

I thought of you because:

_____

_____

_____

_____

The action I'll take
because of this is:

_____

_____

_____

_____

_____

You were on my mind.

_____

I thought of you because:

_____

_____

_____

The action I'll take
because of this is:

_____

_____

_____

_____

You were on my mind.

_____

I thought of you because:

_____

_____

_____

The action I'll take
because of this is:

_____

_____

_____

_____

You were on my mind.

_____

I thought of you because:

_____

_____

_____

The action I'll take
because of this is:

_____

_____

_____

_____

You were on my mind.

_____

I thought of you because:

_____

_____

_____

_____

The action I'll take
because of this is:

_____

_____

_____

_____

_____

You were on my mind.

_____

I thought of you because:

_____

_____

_____

_____

The action I'll take
because of this is:

_____

_____

_____

_____

You were on my mind.

_____

I thought of you because:

_____

_____

_____

_____

The action I'll take
because of this is:

_____

_____

_____

_____

_____

You were on my mind.

_____

I thought of you because:

_____
_____
_____
_____

The action I'll take
because of this is:

_____
_____
_____
_____

You were on my mind.

_____

I thought of you because:

_____

_____

_____

_____

The action I'll take
because of this is:

_____

_____

_____

_____

_____

You were on my mind.

_____

I thought of you because:

_____
_____
_____

The action I'll take
because of this is:

_____
_____
_____
_____

You were on my mind.

_____

I thought of you because:

_____
_____
_____
_____

The action I'll take
because of this is:

_____
_____
_____
_____
_____

You were on my mind.

_____

I thought of you because:

_____

_____

_____

The action I'll take
because of this is:

_____

_____

_____

_____

You were on my mind.

_____

I thought of you because:

_____

_____

_____

The action I'll take
because of this is:

_____

_____

_____

_____

_____

You were on my mind.

_____

I thought of you because:

_____

_____

_____

The action I'll take
because of this is:

_____

_____

_____

_____

You were on my mind.

_____

I thought of you because:

_____

_____

_____

The action I'll take
because of this is:

_____

_____

_____

_____

_____

You were on my mind.

_____

I thought of you because:

_____

_____

_____

_____

The action I'll take
because of this is:

_____

_____

_____

_____

You were on my mind.

_____

I thought of you because:

_____

_____

_____

The action I'll take
because of this is:

_____

_____

_____

_____

_____

You were on my mind.

_____

I thought of you because:

_____

_____

_____

The action I'll take
because of this is:

_____

_____

_____

_____

You were on my mind.

_____

I thought of you because:

_____

_____

_____

_____

The action I'll take
because of this is:

_____

_____

_____

_____

_____

You were on my mind.

_____

I thought of you because:

_____

_____

_____

The action I'll take
because of this is:

_____

_____

_____

_____

You were on my mind.

_____

I thought of you because:

_____

_____

_____

_____

The action I'll take
because of this is:

_____

_____

_____

_____

_____

You were on my mind.

_____

I thought of you because:

_____

_____

_____

The action I'll take
because of this is:

_____

_____

_____

_____

_____

You were on my mind.

_____

I thought of you because:

_____

_____

_____

_____

The action I'll take
because of this is:

_____

_____

_____

_____

_____

You were on my mind.

_____

I thought of you because:

_____

_____

_____

_____

The action I'll take
because of this is:

_____

_____

_____

_____

_____

You were on my mind.

_____

I thought of you because:

_____

_____

_____

_____

The action I'll take
because of this is:

_____

_____

_____

_____

_____

You were on my mind.

_____

I thought of you because:

_____

_____

_____

_____

The action I'll take
because of this is:

_____

_____

_____

_____

_____

You were on my mind.

_____

I thought of you because:

_____

_____

_____

_____

The action I'll take
because of this is:

_____

_____

_____

_____

You were on my mind.

_____

I thought of you because:

_____

_____

_____

_____

The action I'll take
because of this is:

_____

_____

_____

_____

_____

You were on my mind.

_____

I thought of you because:

_____

_____

_____

The action I'll take
because of this is:

_____

_____

_____

_____

You were on my mind.

_____

I thought of you because:

_____

_____

_____

_____

The action I'll take
because of this is:

_____

_____

_____

_____

_____

You were on my mind.

_____

I thought of you because:

_____

_____

_____

_____

The action I'll take
because of this is:

_____

_____

_____

_____

_____

You were on my mind.

_____

I thought of you because:

_____
_____
_____
_____

The action I'll take
because of this is:

_____
_____
_____
_____
_____

You were on my mind.

_____

I thought of you because:

_____

_____

_____

The action I'll take
because of this is:

_____

_____

_____

_____

_____

You were on my mind.

_____

I thought of you because:

_____
_____
_____

The action I'll take
because of this is:

_____
_____
_____
_____
_____

You were on my mind.

_____

I thought of you because:

_____

_____

_____

_____

The action I'll take
because of this is:

_____

_____

_____

_____

_____

You were on my mind.

_____

I thought of you because:

_____

_____

_____

The action I'll take
because of this is:

_____

_____

_____

_____

_____

You were on my mind.

_____

I thought of you because:

_____

_____

_____

_____

The action I'll take
because of this is:

_____

_____

_____

_____

_____

You were on my mind.

_____

I thought of you because:

_____

_____

_____

_____

The action I'll take
because of this is:

_____

_____

_____

_____

_____

You were on my mind.

_____

I thought of you because:

_____

_____

_____

_____

The action I'll take
because of this is:

_____

_____

_____

_____

_____

You were on my mind.

_____

I thought of you because:

_____

_____

_____

_____

The action I'll take
because of this is:

_____

_____

_____

_____

You were on my mind.

_____

I thought of you because:

_____

_____

_____

The action I'll take
because of this is:

_____

_____

_____

_____

You were on my mind.

_____

I thought of you because:

_____

_____

_____

_____

The action I'll take
because of this is:

_____

_____

_____

_____

KIM ROGNE (www.KimRogne.com) is the CEO and founder of For The Love Of, a personal and professional development company. She is a Keynote and Motivational Speaker, Leadership and Entrepreneurial Trainer, Respected Thought Leader in the Mindset Space, and #1 Bestselling Author.

Kim spent 25 years in sales, brokerage management, and recruiting in the Real Estate industry and she is prolific business and real estate investor. She has personally worked with hundreds of business owners from ntry-level through sale of business and spent 7 years as CEO of a multi-million-dollar brokerage filled with hundreds of independent business owners with unique needs.

When Kim walks into a new or changing business or when she steps in front of crowds of high achievers or rooms of growth-minded entrepreneurs, she immediately wants to help those professionals to succeed, live on purpose, and intentionally find a fulfilling balance in all of the areas of their lives.

Kim transitioned smoothly out of the Real Estate space to a highly-sought and successful coaching and speaking business when she began For The Love Of in 2023. The purpose of her company is: To Inspire, Empower, and Promote Action So That You Can Live Your Best For The Love Of Life.

From her website, you can join Kim's online communities, hire her for speaking or coaching, access her digital library, download her business model library, buy her Amazon-available titles, schedule a phone call or virtual meet up, or take dvantage of communications, offers, and opportunities to live your own best For The Love Of life. You will find this wife, mother, friend, voracious learner, and life adventurer to be an immediate spark and motivator in your life.

BONUS! Kim looks forward to continuing to share resources with you and the best places for you to get my most immediately available digital journals, business models, discounts, and downloadables is to visit my website.

www.KimRogne.com

Working with Kim on the *Love Of Journaling"*
books was her sister, friend, and publishing
director. Reji Laberje. Reji, who also writes
as Jeri Shepherd and Maggie McMahon under
the Red Writes Books label can be found at:
www.RedWritesBooks.com

Others

"You are supported."